Damaged But Not Broken

MY TESTIMONY

Krystal Galatia Steward

Copyright © 2016 Krystal Galatia Steward

All rights reserved. Contents and/or covers may not be reproduced in whole or in part in any form without the express written consent of the Author or Publisher. This includes stored in a retrieval system, or transmitted in any form or means, for example but not limited to; photocopying, recording, electronic copying etc., other than purchased as an e-book.

Printed in the United States of America.

Front & back cover inspired and designed by Krystal Galatia Steward. All photos are the property of Krystal Galatia Steward

DEDICATION

I would like to dedicate my book to all the women and young ladies who have struggled through ups and downs and felt that there was no one around to understand nor see their frown...

Just know that God will turn that frown around...

WHERE THERE IS A WILL...

Where there is a will there is definitely a way,
so just know and trust that you will succeed and
overcome someday
God will guide you, he will see you through because
he trusts in you and believes in you

He will show you the way, the right way
because there is a better day
so thank God each and every day for all that comes your way

The entire contents of this book was written by Krystal Galatia Steward and is a reflection of some of the experiences that she has endured and witnessed throughout her life.

TABLE OF CONTENTS

ABOUT ME

Cured_____1
Summertime_____2, 3, 4
In The Beginning_____5
Humble Me_____6
Modelkstew_____7
Lord Knows Best_____8
Nine to Five_____9

FOR KEYAIR

My Heart_____11
Struggle Like Me_____12
Yell & Scream_____13

LIFE

The Game of Life_____15
Only Time Will
Tell What Lies Ahead____16
You Think You Know____17

FAITH & FEAR

Jesus_____19
Give Me Strength_____20
Never Let
Them Break You_____21
Abandonment_____22
Dear Lord_____23
Damage Me Not_____24

GOOD GIRL, WRONG GUY

He Was _____ 26
Who's to Blame _____ 27
DV Isn't For Me _____ 28, 29
Betrayal _____ 30
Same Story! _____ 31
How Could You _____ 32, 33
Emotional Rollercoaster ___ 34
Move On! _____ 35
Wake-up Call _____ 36
Manipulation _____ 37
The Proof
Will Set You Free _____ 38
Held High _____ 43
The End _____ 44
History _____ 45

LOVE OR LUST

This & That _____ 47
Liar Liar _____ 48
Not For Me _____ 49
Differences _____ 50
Worth It _____ 51

OPPOSITES ATTRACT

Inebriation _____ 53
Mistaken _____ 54, 55

NOT THE ONE FOR ME

Deserve vs. Preserve _____ 57
Wifey _____ 58
Afraid of The Dark _____ 59
Think Back _____ 60
Love Thyself
& Know Thy Worth _____ 61
My Life _____ 62

THE MAN FOR ME
Standards_____64
Enthuse Me_____65
My Security_____66
Love, Lust & Trust_____67
Glad Over Bad_____68
My Prince_____69

INSECURITIES
Head to Toe_____71
Cringe_____72
I Hate My Weight_____73

DEPRESSION
Wake-up_____75
When My Day Comes___76
Bigger & Better Place___77
No More Desire_____78
Please Stop_____79
Stronger Than They Know_80

GUARDIAN ANGEL
Flatline_____82
Golden Gates_____83
Fly_____84
Miss You_____85

DEATH
My Guy_____87, 88
Memories_____89
#34_____90
What a Day_____91
Encouraging_____92
More Than a Friend___93
Traffic Light_____94

RESPECT

Focus_____96
More Unity,
Less Brutality_____97
Unity & Positivity_____98

SANITY & STUPIDITY

Words_____100
Forget Me Not_____101
Under Oath_____102
Dis-respect Me Not_____103
Commissary_____104

RECOGNITION

To My Parents_____106
For Martina_____107
For Pat_____108
For Dre_____109

THOUGHTS

MY JOURNEY

Realize_112, 113, 114, & 115
When I Go_____116

Damaged But Not Broken

ACKNOWLEDGMENTS

First & foremost I would like to thank God...

To my grandparents who made my life possible by bringing my parents into the world, you all are my foundation and I love you all very much...

To my mom who gave me everything, even the things I didn't need, that's why for you I would do anything...

To my dad who can make me real mad and at the same time make me real glad, Stew baby is my main squeeze, he keeps me at ease...

To my brother the MCP also known as my big brother Lee, my homey, my ace, no one can ever take your place...

To my son, my sunshine, my world, my life, you give me a purpose and a reason to keep breathing...

To my stepdad, my second dad who makes me real proud and I say that loud, the one who never takes a break and always puts his life at stake...

To my stepmom, my second mom who has always picked me up when I was down, who laughs at my jokes when I'm being a clown and for that I am proud to have you as my second mom...

Damaged But Not Broken

ABOUT ME...

"Judge me not by my appearance, judge me by my interference"

-Krystal Steward

CURED

I had epilepsy as a baby but through prayers and faith my mom said I had my last seizure at eight

I don't remember much except the cherry flavored medicine called Phenobarbital and that is all

I started having headaches at an early age but as long as my seizures have ceased, then I'm at peace

SUMMER TIME

Childhood memories, growing up in the hood, when life was all good

Sometimes I wish I was a kid again and could replay all the fun things I did

My grandma would say "come fix yo plate" and then we would try to stay wake and wait for my cousin to come home, but he was always coming in extra late

My grandma would say girl that Roach ain't bothering you and that mouse ain't studding you, I'm shame of you, acting like that bug was gone hurt you

My grandma would give me $5 to walk to the liquor store and grab her some "squares" now days, a party store owner wouldn't even dare, selling nicotine to a 10 year old wouldn't be smart

To a kid, the hood didn't exist, it was a place where they lived, it was there nest, although to others it was known as a mess but to us kids it was all we knew

Growing up with my grandma I was blessed, she was the best

Our family was very friendly, we were known and loved by many, and my cousins were appreciated and respected by plenty, the fellas knew not to look my way because my cousins weren't having it, they didn't play

SUMMER TIME cont'd

Gunfire was few, far and between or at least that's what it seemed to an innocent kid who didn't know what those sounds really mean

Seeing the police drive down the street didn't bother me, but little did I know they must've been looking for some**BODY**, but I didn't miss a beat, dodgeball was more important to me

When the streetlights came on, my grandma said "you better be home" or you gone feel this belt on yo backside but I knew she was lying because often times I'd just give her a line about how I didn't know because the lights didn't show but all along I was telling a tale because I wanted to stay out and play tag with my pals

Ms. Laney was the penny candy lady, those were the days, I used to have candy for lunch, dinner and sometimes brunch, I didn't need much, because 25cents was just enough to give me a perfect candy rush not to mention the ice cream truck

Popsicles were 4inches thick and only 50cents

Breakfast time was a treat, every morning we would have eggs, grits and some type of meat, whether bacon or ham and toast with jam

My uncle would come and visit, and often bring KFC, oh what a treat, it was always a feast, we would all laugh, mingle and eat and then I would drift off to sleep

SUMMER TIME cont'd

My dad taught me how to iron and make a mean crease
in just about anything because back then that's how your clothes were
expected to be, neat and wrinkle free

I once saw a puppy walking down the street with no apparent family,
brown fur, green eyes, most beautiful
thing I had ever seen, I begged my grandma to let me keep him/her
and she conferred but it had to stay outdoors, oh how I loved him/her
but it was only a blur because someone soon took him/her

My cousins were like my big brother's, they would watch me like no
other

My report card was like a paycheck, I used to get all A's and once I
showed the fellas…I would be paid, I had it made

Those were the days…

IN THE BEGINNING

I started working at the age of 14

I had to help my mom make ends meet

It was hard not always having heat, and sometimes not

even having a bite to eat

Sometimes not having proper shoes to

walk down the street

But in the end, it made me the strong, independent woman

that I am today and for that I will always be thankful and

forever grateful...

HUMBLE ME

Humble is what I have to be,

humble is what I was taught to be,

boasting is not where it's at for me.

I'm no better than the girl next to me,

in back of me, or in front of me.

I'm just Krystal you see, nothing more than a small town girl who

yearns for more like her, him or them.

We all want more but we need to fight to achieve it so we can retrieve

it because a dream is only a mere thought if you don't seek it

MODELKSTEW

Modeling was never about the competition for me,
the fame,
or who's pretty enough to stay in the game
It was about showing that I could maintain
and keep a humble brain
because at the end of the day I'm still the same
Lights, Camera, Action,
I'm still gone be me no matter who's watching me, whether it be for photography or just to walk down the street I'm still gone be me
A picture will never define me
Fashion shows, I did that
Crowns I won those
Trophy's I mount those
Photos, I got many of those
Audition's, I rocked em
But in the end I decided a college degree was much more intriguing to me so before you question my integrity and whether or not modeling was reality for me make sure you got a pen and a pad because you gone wanna take notes
The modeling game ain't no joke
You think it's all glitz and glam but on the other hand you might be posing for pervs who only wanna see yo curves
My posing game was sweet, I was quite unique but my walking game was on fleek that's why the photographers hired me and the designers requested me but in the end that college degree seemed more promising to me
So here I am certified and degree bound as I wear my modeling crown

LORD KNOWS BEST

The Dr. diagnosed me with fibrocystic breast disease

Oh Lord, how could this be, what does this mean?

I've cried and I've cried, I'm on my knees
Lord please, rid me of this disease and free me from cancer and anything else

WHY ME?

Lord help me and guide me

because you are the ruler of all things

and through you I am and will be free

from any and all things

NINE TO FIVE

I work, work, work, and in the end I'm always broke, broke, broke because my bills are my pimps and I'm stuck on the strip everyday trying to make a dollar out of 25 cents by working 9-5 because I gotta get by but in the end I got a bed under my butt, a fridge for my food, water for my washing, heat for my feet and a roof for my residence so although my pimps may be mean, I give them what they fiend, my hard earned green because without them this life would be much more mean

For Keyair

MY HEART

You are my world
you are my heart
you give me hope
you give me faith
you give me the strength
to take a breath each and everyday

and I love you more than words could ever say

Thank you Lord for my son because he is the beat

that makes my heart

continue to start

STRUGGLE LIKE ME

My son never had to eat a syrup sandwich like me or wished a cracker was a burger and fries
My son never been evicted and put out on the street like me, my mama worked hard but couldn't always make ends meat
My son never had to catch a bus like me, in the dead of winter, walking down the street with raggedy shoes on my feet which is why I bought my 1st, 2nd, 3rd, 4th, 5th and 6th car and I work twice as hard so he won't have to starve
My son never had his toys took away from strangers while he looked on with sadness and anger while his mama cried to the landlord I'll pay you later
My son will never know struggle like me
I slept on a box spring and although it was brief, to this day my back gives me grief, but my son will always sleep comfortably, because he will never know the struggle like me
Don't get me wrong, my mama was the best, I just had to get this off my chest
My mama did her best, through sickness and in health
We weren't poor forever but I can never say never, so I know struggle and it was a hard life test but my mama was the best and through it all we stayed blessed
My struggle taught me to work hard and stay on the grind so my son won't have to do no time because I vow that he will never know struggle and my hard work will keep him out of trouble

YELL & SCREAM

Sometimes I **YELL** and even **SCREAM** but I want my son to know I don't mean to be mean, I just want him to know I would do anything for him to see how much he truly means to me

Sometimes I have to **YELL** and **SCREAM** to be what I need him to be and to see what I need him to see because one day he will grow up to be the young man that I destined and raised him to be

Life may be full of misery but I want him to grow up and find the luxury because any fantasy can become a reality

I tell him seek and Ye shall find, your heart and mind move based on your time so in due time you will be just fine

Life

"Life is what you make it, if you want better you have to seek it"

-Krystal Steward

THE GAME OF LIFE

Life to me is in many ways comparable to the board game known as Monopoly:

For example, when you play Monopoly, every time we roll the dice we wonder what we're going to land on. Are we going to land on anything good that is worth our while like Boardwalk or Park Place, or will we land on the Go to Jail box?

In life we strive to live comfortably and be happy, no one wants to be poor and unhappy. Life is full of what if's... Will we get rich, will our bills get paid, will we be able to make our rent or mortgage payment on time, will we find a job, etc. We go through life with so many worries, concerns, and stressors.

In the game of Monopoly the object is to not give up, keep playing, and keep going until the end, until you can't play anymore. The problem is you don't know when the end is, so it makes you wonder and makes you curious, will I live or die, win or lose? When you play monopoly you never know when the game is going to end, it could last for hours, or days, similar to life, you just never know what life will bring your way nor do you know when the end is coming.

ONLY TIME WILL TELL WHAT LIES AHEAD

Don't cherish tomorrow,

cherish today

No one knows what tomorrow is

destined to bring accept GOD

Thank GOD for today before you thank

him for tomorrow

Take life day by day

Don't jump forward to the future when

you're still in the present

Don't jump ahead of time, let it stay ahead of you

YOU THINK YOU KNOW

You think you know but you have no idea

what I've been through for the

last 30 plus years...

The tears,

I've cried many tears

my fears,

I've had many fears

I've been hurting for soooo long, toooo long,

many, many years

I've cried these tears and tried to fight my fears alone

for far too long...

There's no one near to see my tears

nor hear my fears...

UNTIL NOW

Faith and Fear…

"When I go home at night I feel so alone, in my own home, I'm all alone, my mind is in a constant zone of its own"

-Krystal Steward

JESUS!

JESUS…JESUS…JESUS
I ask that you please place your hands upon me and stop whatever negative force is mocking me because they are trying to stop me, they don't want to see me succeed so I ask that you please place your loving hands around me and walk with me because they are trying to surround me but they will never get through you because they are afraid of you

GIVE ME STRENGTH

I asked the Lord to give me strength to not stress over the thing's people do and the thing's I cannot understand and the Lord said to me
"If there is no pain, there is no crime"

Meaning if you are not bruised, beaten, or bleeding, then you are ok and will be ok. People's words and actions may hurt you, for they know not what they say and do.

So I say to these people...you may not care about your wrong doings now but you will come judgment day so as of today I will no longer allow your stupidity to affect my sanity, because your stupidity will affect you in the end…

NEVER LET THEM BREAK YOU

I love to be loved

I like to be liked

I hate to be hated

And I now know as I didn't before

not everyone will love you

not everyone will like you

some will even hate you

and may even try to shake you

but just remember to never let them break you
Because GOD made you…

ABANDONMENT

My mother, my hero, my buddy, my backbone

where did you go, how could you leave me?

You left us, you deserted us

you ran away, you just up and left the state with no

trace

your sickness, your illness, your life,

your independence

I understand, I do but in some ways I don't

I miss you, I need you but through it all

I will continue to hope and pray that GOD will

bring you back home safe someday...

DEAR LORD

My mother had a pain in her chest,

they found a lump in her breast

I'm so upset

I do my best to stay strong

But in my head I feel so alone

So I pray, and I pray and I say to the highest power

Lord please don't take my mother...

give her cover

heal her

mend her

make her stronger than ever before but Lord
whatever you do, please don't take my mother
because Dear Lord I need my mother

DAMAGE ME NOT

You thought you could damage my dreams and stop my goals with all these obstacles

Well devil, you can stay in the heat because I'd rather be out in the cold than down in hell where you should be

So I'm gone keep climbing to the top because my motivation don't stop

Good Girl Wrong Guy

HE WAS

When I first saw him I thought he was fake

Then, I soon realized, he just had to be my mate

Soon we grew into a love I had never knew

Later we were split apart,

and we departed with a broken heart

WHO'S TO BLAME

I feel weak

I can't speak

I can't think

I hardly even eat

I feel ashamed

I feel insane

I feel as if I'm the one to blame

But yet he's the one who's really insane

and the one who deserves all the blame...

DV ISN'T FOR ME

A disagreement turned into a fight,
a fight for my life
A fight that would unfortunately change my life
Your hurting me, your trying to kill me, aren't you?
What's wrong with you, how could you?
My parents aren't home, my brother is home but is unfortunately dead to the world so I'm all alone
I wanna scream, I wanna cry but I have to be strong in order to make it through this night
I beg and I plead but there is no sympathy
You continue to hit me and threaten me continuously…Oh LORD, why me
I decide to fight back and I am eventually able to grab a knife and say "STAY BACK"
Wrong move, why did I do that, you now have the knife and I am once again begging and pleading for my life
Please LORD, end this night

DV ISN'T FOR ME cont'd

Thank GOD, I am finally able to break free and call the police, I can no longer take nor tolerate your abuse
I have bruises, I have scars so why am I being taken away in a police car?

I called the police to come get this creep before he really succeeds at killing me and they got me in shackles and cuffs like I did some stuff
Wow I guess the police really just don't give a you know what
I was taught that the police were here to protect you, not to neglect you
Only 18,
I couldn't understand what any of this means
I had a 3 day jail-cation and 2 years of probation, they took all my motivation and stimulation,
I really wish this was just my imagination!

BETRAYAL

My parents took you in and allowed us to live in sin.
They felt sorry for you, your family and your friends didn't want any part
of you because they knew the truth about the real you.
My mother adored you,
but now
she's afraid of you and what you might do
my family accepted you, now they can't stand you, they cringe at the
thought of you...
Who Are You?

SAME STORY

We fought like cats and dogs constantly.

This isn't love, this isn't how a relationship should be...
You punk me, I punk you
You push me, I push you
You hit me, I hit you
I HATE you,

I can't stand you
We kiss, we make up
We hug, we're back in love
We sleep, we wake up
New day...
same story

HOW COULD YOU!

Everyone thought we would get married someday, (especially you) walk down the aisle and birth our first child

High school sweethearts, two peas in a pod, we were inseparable, we were in love, we were best friends, almost like twins

Then something happened that caused you to change...

your illness took over

How could this be, your illness has caused you to turn on me, your thoughts have become distorted and as a result our first child was aborted

Only eighteen, I had to do it alone because your insanity wouldn't allow you to be there for me at my most desperate time of need and grief

You aren't the same, you've changed, you have become completely insane and as a result I have to move on

Sadly enough, years later when the next girl comes around and soon claims to be pregnant with your child, you quickly but reluctantly say "I DO" and walk her down the aisle

HOW COULD YOU!

HOW COULD YOU! Cont'd

Well the jokes on you, three months later you find out it isn't true, oops she lied to you...HOW COULD SHE!

She surely played you!

Now for the last eight years you have been chasing after me, begging for a chance to re-impregnate me and say "I DO"
SHAME ON YOU!

EMOTIONAL ROLLERCOASTER

I have been embarrassed and ashamed for far too long,
everyone knows you're insane, especially me, so why do I feel the need
to provide you with my help and my sympathy when truthfully and
quite honestly what have you ever done for me besides bring me grief...
I feel sorry for you, I really do, but every time I felt sorry for you,
I tried to help you and be there for you and every time I tried to help
you it fell through...

I helped you once, twice, far too many times and then it backfires and
I'm stuck saying "WHY" why did I even try? You put your hands on
me enough times, but when you did it in front of my child, that was
definitely the last time. You bragged about putting your hands on
others, even your own mother.

I hope you are never able to ever hurt another
You threatened to kill me so many times and you attempted to kill me
enough times for me to realize that there will be no more times...

MOVE ON!

Your threats, your stalking, your excessive phone calling.
When will it stop, when will it end,
because I can no longer pretend
This is not cool, and definitely not okay
Something needs to be done, something should be said.
I cannot deal with this for not another day,
this is insane, this is absurd.
When will he learn
You say you need me but you really need Jesus, a higher power is the
only one who can cure your heartache and sorrow
You continue to say you will never find another quite like me nor will
you ever love another as much as you love me and yes, I agree
So you best leave me be and start on your quest to search for someone
similar but not quite me because it is obvious
to me that you are not the one for me

WAKE-UP CALL

When your disorders take over Satan comes out and when he comes out there's no way out until you snap back into reality and realize

"Oh My GOD"

I did it again but sadly by then everyone is afraid of you and what you might do so everyone runs and hides from you because they are petrified of you and so are you!

Not even two weeks before the last time that you jumped on me, I had

a nightmare and envisioned everything that you did to me

For years you have been my nightmare, you have been the monster

that has haunted me in my dreams as well as in my reality…

All these years I have ignored the clues and looked passed all the cues

but starting today I am awake, wide awake!

MANIPULATION

You used to tell me you would always find me even if I left the state, you told me you would always find my trace no matter the time or place. You used to drive past my place and even walk past and pace until you saw someone come in or out of my space and ask them was I doing ok.

You would call me a thousand times until I picked up the line, then you would tell me how you tried to commit suicide.

You would cry and weep and manipulate me to think that I was at fault for all that you did to me, making me feel guilty, from the time you overdosed on pills because I refused to come chill to the time you crashed your car into the light pole on Washtenaw, you blamed it all on me because I was no longer willing to be a part of your misery…I'm so tired of this insanity

THE PROOF WILL SET YOU FREE

The first PPO didn't scare you
A year was only enough to dare you

The second PPO did more than scare you
14 years, I dare you!

The judge saw proof of what I been through and she definitely scared you, her decision was based on truth through the paper trail that will eventually lead you straight to jail if you continue to try to bring me hell

All that you have done to me has given me the courage and the strength to write this book because I finally decided enough was enough and I thank the Judicial system for finally having my back because violence against woman is truly whack and that is a fact

**I would like to give a special Thank you to Officer Sharrock.
I cannot express my gratitude and appreciation enough for all of your help, advice and concern.
I thank God for officers like you and for you being one of the officers at the scene that night.**

**Thank you so much from the bottom of our hearts,
from myself & my son**

Damaged But Not Broken

Thank You Dr. Stew

You are the big reason why I became stronger on 5, 9, 2010 which was Mother's Day. After talking with you that night which I only remember bits and pieces, I finally realize that it was you I was on the phone with. In that frame of mind normally whoever I'm on the phone with would hang up the phone but you did stay on the phone with me for a while. After that night I got tired of how I was living not having nothing from money to pay bills and other things for myself, to not having someone special to talk to or cuddle with on the July instead of being miserable drinking everyday. I just want to tell you I know I put you through a lot in that last 10 years of dealing with you and I want to tell you I'm sorry. Life is still going on for the both of us and from this point on I just want to make up for those terrible times we had in the past. I want to tell you I love you with all my heart and I will make up for the past if you give me the time and day to do so. I apologize for not being there for you when I made the immature decision to abort the child. I regret making that decision till this day and even though Keyser is not biologically mine, I don't look at it like that. I love him like he is mine and hope that I can be there for him throughout his life watching him grow into a grown adult. Financially I'm not that shit right now but it will be a matter of time before I get there. I really appreciate you being there for me in the lowest time of my life and I promise you will be blessed from God and me with great things. Just Watch And See!!!

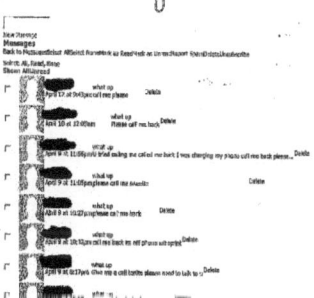

Damaged But Not Broken

My THOUGHTS
HOLD YOU TENDERLY,
MY HEART TREASURES YOU,
AND MY LOVE
EMBRACES YOU...
FOREVER.

From You Ex-Boo.
Love You forever even though
You and Mine.

♡ + ♡ = ♡ One Day

Damaged But Not Broken

HELD HIGH

I used to look over my shoulders

but now I walk with my head held high,

walking with pride not worried about looking from side to side

I'd rather die with my head held high looking to the sky then my head hung low facing below where you are planning to go

THE END

You've hurt me more than most will ever know

you've done horrible things over the last 9 years,

tragic things that most would find hard to fathom or even believe

you and I both know that you have issues

and through it all GOD has been my witness...

HISTORY

We may have history, unfortunately...

This history has caused me much misery...

This history ends now and for eternity so

GOODBYE,

GOOD LUCK,

& GOD BLESS YOU!

Love or Lust...

"He told me this he told me that, but none of it was a fact, he was full of craph, all of it was a trap, regardless of how I had his back"

-Krystal Steward

THIS & THAT

He told me this, he told me that

But half of what he said wasn't all that

Half of what he said

was what I wanted to hear

And the other half was

what he thought I should hear

They tell us they love us

They tell us they need us

But truth is they lust for us

and really could care less about us

LIAR LIAR

He lied to you, he lied to me, I didn't know about you nor did you know about me so contrary to what you might think, he is not what you think, a king this man will never be because he betrayed you and me, he was trying to wife me, so it seemed, wined and dined me, hosted and boasted me, at my crib every night kissing, hugging and loving me, and hype me up to think he was true to me, I was his lady he was my man, everything seemed so perfect and planned but his life beknost to me was that of someone who was unknown to me, a real life rebel in disguise who could undress you with his eyes

He seemed so kind and sweet but all the while was playing games and in the midst of it I became just another one of his side thangs because to him I wasn't the real thang I was only a play thang and a piece to his board game

Now our children are forever tied and that can't be denied which is why I forgave what you did to us that day on the road even though my baby (who was only 2) and I were innocent and had no idea about any of this, the one you really wanted denied even knowing you until years later when I found out the truth and til this day you still have hate in you regardless of the truth which is that I really didn't know about you but I hope that one day we can be friends and you can see why your boys love me just as much as I love them

NOT FOR ME

Immaturity, infidelity and negativity
Keep that all away from me
You did this to me
Made me feel so cheap
Like a piece of meat
When all I really wanted was for it to be you and me
This pain runs so deep like a dog in heat
So now I stay where it's safe for me
Everybody is not here for me or there for me like they claim to be

DIFFERENCES

Love to you means lust

Love to me means trust

Telling lies is the best policy in your eyes

Telling the truth is honesty in my mind

Cheating is a game to you

Cheating to me is being unfaithful and untrue

Soon you will see, because you will never find another as true as me

WORTH IT

Woman make the world go round but it's up to men to make us feel worthwhile but instead they steadily jumping around because it's more woman then men to be found…

Opposites Attract

INEBRIEATION

I fell for a man that was younger than me
Something that was out of ordinary for me
Because it was not in my personality
He was head over hills for me but he was a kid to me
Having fun, making love, spending time was a game to me until he became intriguing to me
He proved he was a man to me
And he had true love for me but he had a situation that couldn't be mistaken nor forsaken
His intensions wasn't bad, his situation was sad and for that he will always be known as my complicated inebriation
I grew to love his flaws and all and he knew how to walk through my walls and conquer my trust through his love and lust
I showed him what a real woman could do because my love and affection became true

MISTAKEN

He possessed me with his positivity and maturity and allowed me to see pass his insecurities and made me a part of his extended family...he was my best friend and my main man, a relationship so it seemed, in love maybe, a friendship for damn sure but a game of love and war is what it became more and more

We fought because of our lust but it only caused disgust, we used to have so much trust, how could we be so tough and give this all up but then we always make up. Best friends was our name but lovers was what we became and having sex was our game but in the end it only caused anguish and pain, I feel like I'm going insane and he says he feels the same, he needs me in his life, I would make a great wife, I make him whole but this other situation caused for immediate mediation in order for him to be around for his seed but I stay in the shadow while he lives that life out loud but he calls me constantly and I'm his everything and all he needs but honestly it feels like I'm not anything even after all he's did for me, that's why I call It Complicated because Betrayal ultimately became his name.
In the end I had to give him resignation for his admissions because he was so persistent which ultimately seemed like bad intentions trying to act like everything was cool when he admitted he had been unfaithful and untrue regarding what we had been through so now the glue that held what we had, became loose and I stepped

MISTAKEN cont'd

away giving him an ultimatum
but the glue stayed loose and I was stuck saying...
"Damn You" and once again in life I had to repeat "How Could You"
But I wished him the best and Said God Bless, but I will no longer be a part of your quest, I'd wished I never got involved in this mess
He says he thinks and dreams of me constantly, his mind won't get rid of me, he says he loves me unconditionally but his life right now doesn't allow for him to be with me like he desires to be
because his life is complicated and full of misery and
when he's with me he forgets it all but I guess misery is more inviting than me because when he leaves, he's right back at miseries door
because it loves his company...

Not The One For Me

DESERVE VS. PRESERVE

I fall for the ones I shouldn't and I ignore the ones I shouldn't
The ones I like got lives full of mess and stress and I'm stuck trying to help their inner happiness manifest
The ones I don't, show me luxury but I'm too busy looking back at the ones that cause misery and the others are calling out to me saying "Why won't you fall for me" I wanna give you a life full of happiness and luxury but unfortunately my attraction is with misery, luxury is what I deserve but misery is what I often preserve

WIFEY

The ones who have tried to wife me, weren't right for me or my life you see

They may have loved me and adored me but they damn sure weren't for me

They tried to force me to see that they were the one for me but in all actuality they weren't right for me but I understand, to them, they are my ideal man but to me, they are not at all what I have planned

AFRAID OF THE DARK

I give these dudes bad news when they want to enthuse me and not use me, they want to love me and care for me, they say you need to choose, you shouldn't use because you will only loose but I'm sorry they must be confused because I once was the one that was used and abused when all I wanted was a walk in the park and a rose for my heart but often times I was left in the dark so now I take my time driving to the park because my heart is now afraid of the dark so it no longer parks...

THINK BACK

They didn't realize what they had until I was gone, because they was

playing games all along

Now they stuck writing me love songs

Leaving me texts, forgetting they my ex

You had chance after chance, and true love didn't manifest

The past is the past

When I'm done, I'm done

And when I'm gone, I'm gone

So I don't wanna hear yo sad song

So move on, you had your chance, and that's a fact

All this nonsense is really whack

So I'm gone leave you in yo tracks and allow you to think back

LOVE THY SELF & KNOW THY WORTH

Why should I settle for less knowing I deserve nothing but the best

Like the saying goes; "I can do bad all by myself."

You used me and abused me but all that did was make you loose me so please don't try to enthuse me wit yo lies and yo cries

I didn't need you, you needed me but you couldn't handle me; a real chic, independent on my own 2 feet and that's all I'll ever be you see, so PEACE!
And don't call me

MY LIFE

I am not damaged because I chose to be, I'm damaged because of what became of me and what happened to me

I been hurt enough to know that if it's not working I got to go

My heart is sacred so I can no longer allow you to break it nor shake it

When Mr. Right comes along I will embrace it

But until then, my life is what I make it

The Man For Me

STANDARDS

The man who is for me may be opposite of me and what I have held
my standards to be
He may be younger than me or even older than me
He may be shorter than me or a few inches taller than me
He may be richer than me or poorer than me trying to get on his feet
He may have a heart of gold much bigger than me
But one thing for sure he must be God fearing and have unconditional
love for me

ENTHUSE ME

I want a dude that will amuse me and enthuse me, do anything not to loose me
Surprise me with a picnic in the park to seal my heart like cupid threw a dart
Give me a rush from his simple touch, make me lust from his manly musk and cause me to blush
That's the kind of love I phene, the kind where making love is like a dream

I want you to send me a text saying "have a good day" and I reply "don't be late when I fix yo plate" then we go out on a date

MY SECURITY

Give me you and I'll give you me but first you got to bust down these walls you see, I can't give you me before I see the intent and impact your trying to make with me, my walls are my security, they keep me safe from the hurt and the pain because I no longer have time for the games, it's such a shame, because love is not meant to be a game

LOVE, LUST & TRUST

Love is love

Lust is lust

Trust is trust

But a must is a must, if you love me, you must trust me and not just lust for me because a must is a must and if I'm gone trust you then I must love you because lust just isn't enough

GLAD OVER BAD

The good times should outweigh the bad
and if they don't then that's just plain sad
and it's time to change plans
because your bad isn't worth my glad
When I'm feeling sad,
you should be making me glad not making me mad

MY PRINCE

I realize that prince charming may not exist
but I want a man that will show me that I exist
Seal his love with a kiss
surprise me,
shower me with gifts,
take me on trips
And show me that true love still exists

Insecurities...

"Confidence & self-esteem are few, far and between when you have so many insecurities"

-Krystal Steward

HEAD TO TOE

I'm insecure from my head to my toe but most people would never know because I try not to let it show but little do they know, I'm not happy with myself from my face to my hair, my lips to my nose, they are out of control, truth be told I can't stand my mold but I have learned to be comfortable with me because I can't hide what people see, so I continue to do me, love me and be who God created me to be

CRINGE

When people stare at me, I wanna cringe because I feel so ugly in my skin
I often feel like an ugly duckling in a pond full of swans, I feel frowned upon
People think I'm confident but I'm total opposite
They say I'm pretty and I say "who me"?
You can't be serious, you must be delirious

I HATE MY WEIGHT

I'm too thin, I'm too small

So I eat, I eat, and I eat

But it's no use

I won't gain any weight

How could this be

It seems that I will be ugly for eternity

I want to be thick, I want to be fat, anything but this

This is a fact...

Depression

"I carry a smile on my face every day but that doesn't mean I'm ok"

-Krystal Steward

WAKE-UP

When I woke up yesterday I didn't like myself

When I woke up today, I hated myself

When I wake up tomorrow I might wanna kill myself

Today I don't feel myself because yesterday was the

day I was supposed to kill myself...

WHEN MY DAY COMES

I live everyday wondering: when my life will end,

where my life will end

All I come to realize is that it will someday and I will

continue to await for that particular day

When my day comes whether I am surprised

or not surprised, I will be ready

What I will leave behind, I don't know, but I will be ready and

that I do know

BIGGER & BETTER PLACE

I'm depressed, I'm stressed because I would like

to take a bigger and better step

to a life filled with happiness

I feel lifeless, I feel weak

I try and stop myself from falling too deep

Someway, someday I will find my way to that bigger

and better place and that will be a great day

NO MORE DESIRE

I was depressed, I didn't wanna live
I felt like people didn't appreciate the things that I did,
it was always give, give, give
My mind was tired, I felt the need to expire, I had no more desire
This world so full of deceit
and all I ever wanted was to be happy and free
My peace of mind was starting to feel more like a waste of time
My motivation was no longer a temptation
Everyone used me and abused me and tried to enthuse me
Gullible I seemed but in all actuality it was the God in me that allowed
me to keep helping those in need because I have a heart of gold and
although many have stolen it, I still control it

Damaged But Not Broken

PLEASE STOP

I'm confused

Why is he doing this?

Is he really doing this?

I can't believe he's doing this!

I try to push him, but he won't budge

I feel pain, I feel blood

This isn't love

I tell him to stop over and over

I thought he was my friend,

that's how our relationship began

but not how it ends because we will be friends never again...

STRONGER THAN THEY KNOW

Sometimes the hurt you feel is so deep, you can't eat or even sleep, you feel it deep and wonder why me, sadness is a pain like no other, it breaks you down mentally, physically and emotionally, the hurt doesn't leave, it stays forever in your heart, your mind and even your soul and little do people know they helped that evil sadness to manifest and live stagnant in your mind, body and soul because they didn't know what they said could have such a toll on your soul

So many people have said and did things to me that have cut extremely deep but it is unknown to them that they have affected me tremendously because I tend to not let it show because I'm stronger than they know

Guardian Angel

FLATLINE____

You look like your sleep but truth is, you're gone for eternity
I wanna shake you to wake you
They say flat line….
but I need more time
I watched you leave but it felt more like a dream
I felt you leave but wished God would bring you back to me
I held your hand, it was cold to the touch, but never the less I would continue to warm it up
Traumatized as I witnessed it all with my own eyes
I watched you die, goodbye but why
I hate the way they took you away
What a horrific way to end my day
This giant white box has me in so much shock,
my world has just stopped!

GOLDEN GATES

I would like to believe that as I held your hand and told you to wait,
you made your way through those golden gates
I felt your hands go from warm to numb so I grabbed you tight but it
was apparent you had given up the fight,
There was no more life because you had went on to follow that
beautiful bright light

FLY

As I sat beside you I prayed that you could stay another day
because I wanted my way
I couldn't bare the thought of losing you
What would I do? What would they do? What would we do?
We need you, I need you but most of all God needs you, he's calling you
So as I cry, I sadly realize…it is time, you must fly my beautiful butterfly but this my angel is not Goodbye…
I will see you again on the other side

My eternal love will never cease because in my heart I know you are at peace…
I love you grandma

MISS YOU

I miss my grandma
I wish I could kiss her
Hold her and hug her
And tell her how much I love her
Sit at the table and tell her about my week, gossip and eat
What a joyous time it would be when I got to visit my grandma after a rough hard week
She would tell me to have a seat and tell her all about my week as we sat and ate KFC then she would drift off to sleep, she was as cute as could be with her rosy pink cheeks
I would say grandma wake up, we're not done catching up and she would say "oh hunny, I'm sorry." and soon drift off again and I would seal her forehead with a tiny kiss until the next time we met up for our weekly catch up

Death

MY GUY

His name was Guy, he died when I was little

They say he was quite a guy, a great guy, a strict guy, a stern guy and sometimes a mean guy

He was an Army vet and he wore his honor pattoned on his chest

My memories of him are scarce but the ones I have I hold close to my heart, he would put me in the Taurus and we would go to DQ for ice cream and to this day I get the same thing so I can keep that memory of you...because Mr. Steward, I may not remember much of you, but Grandad I'll always love you

I know you were good with your hands because you added rooms to your house and oh how I wish you were here to help me with my first house

You may have been rough around the edges to most but you were tender at heart because I remember you sent money to the kids in another country because they were hungry and now I do the same to represent your name

I wish I was there when you were sick to give you a hug and a kiss

I often look at my dad to see if he reminds me of you but I was so young and my memories are not fond enough to know if it's true but I sometimes ask him questions about you

MY GUY cont'd

But one things for sure, him and my uncle act like you
and Byrd definitely favors you

Your Steward blood runs deep because we all have similar qualities and
when we get mad people say that's the Steward blood running deep like
a creek

Just know, I take your name with pride because if it wasn't for you I
wouldn't be alive

RIP My Guy

MEMORIES

I was just a baby when my uncle died so my memories of him are pretty nonexistent but those of my aunt are persistent, she was quite the lady and I was her baby, she was bubbly and fun, I have vague memories of being at her house, I can even drive by and still point it out, I didn't know she was sick, I just wanted my special auntie kiss but after a while I learned it would no longer exist

Dedicated to and in loving memory of
Aunt Jeanette
And
Uncle Vince
R.I.P.

#34

You made me laugh without a doubt
there was something about you that no one feared
because you were such a special friend
even through the thick
as well as the thin....

Dedicated to and in loving memory of Sam
R.I.P.
1983-1999

WHAT A DAY

He died on my 21st birthday
We all cried on my 21st birthday
A special day turned into a bad day
A glad day turned into a sad day
My birthday had become a death day...
because he left this earth on my 21st Birthday...

Dedicated to and in loving memory of
Grandpa Tyree
R.I.P.
1933-2003

ENCOURAGING

You were kind,

you were sweet

your presence was uplifting, your words were encouraging,

your advice will never cease and for that,

you will be remembered for eternity

Dedicated to and in loving memory of
Kent
R.I.P.
1983-2003

MORE THAN A FRIEND

More than a friend
you were someone that I could confide in
no matter the time nor place
you were someone that would give a helping hand
no matter what day and for that
no one will ever take your place
you are gone to a better place....

Dedicated to and in loving memory of
Ronald
R.I.P.
1978-2003

TRAFFIC LIGHT

I was on my way to pick you up but for some reason you wouldn't pick up.

At the traffic light I looked over to my right and an old friend looked over at me…

It was apparent and obvious to me that she was saying SORRY

BUT WHY?

When we pulled over, all I could do was cry because she confirmed for me why you couldn't pick up and my day went from good to bad and now I will forever be sad

-I love you dear friend, my big sis, your smile still exists and I will continue to blow you a kiss as you fly high in the beautiful sky

Dedicated to and in loving memory of
Joycelyn
R.I.P.
1971-2014

Damaged But Not Broken

Respect

FOCUS

Lord gave us life

So why not try and do right

Love one another, don't kill each other

Today is here, so we think tomorrow is near

This poem is dedicated to all who have lost their lives to violence and crime...

MORE UNITY, LESS BRUTALITY

Violence against woman needs to end

We can no longer pretend that this silence is going to win

When will we begin to stand up, speak out, and reach out?

No one steps up, no one speaks up

We need to speak up and shout

STOP!

To the highest mountain top

Because without UNITY
There will continue to be
BRUTALITY
sadly
&
unfortunately

UNITY & POSITIVITY

They're killing us, we're killing us, they mad at us, this world has no trust, we disgrace ourselves and give them more the reason to eliminate us because deep down they hate us, we went from slaves to maids, having a black president didn't put us in the game, it just made them more insane, now there on a constant rampage, a traffic stop is no longer a traffic stop, it's an attempt to show that your black and there not, the white man will always win because in the end we're working with them instead of against them, we shooting up the block while they killing us during routine traffic stops, they killing one of us, we killing two, three and four of us, from Detroit, to LA, from Philly to Chi town and all around the world the gang banging is no good if u wanna stand up for yo hood, you got to walk and represent, and put away the clip because the trigger shouldn't exist at a time like this, United is what we need to be, humble, positive and free, holding hands and chanting

"Yes We Can"

Because without unity we will never see positivity

**Dedicated to all those who have lost their lives during our divide including but not limited to Tamir, 12, Trayvon, 17, Michael, 18, John, 22, Sandra, 28, Dontre, 31, Tanisha, 37, Eric G., 43, Eric H., 44, Walter, 50.
The list continues...**

Sanity & Stupidity

WORDS!

The saying goes "sticks and stones may break my bones but words will never hurt me"...

But in actuality words sometimes hurt a lot more than the scars and bruises because words stick with you, words are not always easily forgotten. Sticks and stones may break our bones but the wounds will eventually heal. Words can never be taken back, because once something is said, it's said. The person who made the comment or statement may eventually forget but the person it was said to may never forget. We sometimes say things to one another without realizing how much of an impact it may have on someone and how hurtful it may be, we may not mean it in a hurtful way but it may be taken and interpreted in a hurtful way. Sometimes the simplest comment can be taken negatively, even if meant as a compliment.

My grandma always said;

"if you don't have anything nice to say, then don't say anything at all"

You never know what someone is going through or has went through and how your words and/or actions may affect them or has affected them so be conscientious of what you say and do to others.

"Treat others as you want to be treated."

FORGET ME NOT

People tend to forget what you do for them,
they often remember a heart that's cold and of stone before they
remember a heart of gold so it seems and so I've been told

But I always remember what was did for me rather than what was told
of me because I know what's true of me

so you believe what you believe, truth be told you know nothing about
me, you think what you think but only I know me truly and I and my
family will love me unconditionally

UNDER OATH

Your jealous of me

You envy me

The saddest part is you don't even know me

How could you go to court, in front of a judge,

raise your right-hand and lie under oath

Sin is obviously your friend

but GOD is my BFF to the end

So what you did will come back again and again because

GOD knows the truth and sadly so do you but regardless

of it all I will pray for you...

DISRESPECT ME NOT

I be damned if I let you dis-respect me

Man I swear people always trying to test me
They wanna step to me because they are often fooled by my size and not my mind
Small things come in big packages
I might be soft-spoken but my voice does not define my mind
So pay more attention to what comes out my mouth because there's no need for me to shout because by the end of the convo you will understand what respect is all about

COMMISSARY

I guess commissary was all it took for my uncle to sell my address and my photo to his adversary

I still got the letters to this day from the guys locked behind the prison gates writing me about how they can't wait to get out and see my true face

How unsafe, how could my uncle do me this way, these guys have seen my face and know where I stay

But then I say, how could he do any of the things he's done, he clearly doesn't understand right from wrong because he has many nieces that he's done wrong to and family that he's hurt along the way but uncle I say to you, through it all I was there for you, because your my uncle and I love you but I sure don't like you and the things you do but I pray that God bless and be with you

Recognition

To My Parents…

Gregory, Karmen, Delores and Shawn, thank you for raising me and sticking by me thus far

You deserve a standing ovation for your consistent positive motivation.

Thank you from the bottom of my heart!

I love you all, much more than words can ever explain!

&

To My God-Mom Durrinda,
Thank you for loving me like your own and for allowing me to be a big sister, something I always wanted to be and I promise to continue to be the best role-model that I can be for Ang & London for my eternity

For Martina

My best friend means the world to me, known her since I was 16 you see, 2 peas in a pod, doesn't matter who's even or odd, opposites we may be but best friends we will always be because she understands me and I understand her, a million miles away but I can still call her and say "Hey, how was your day" no matter the time or how far away, I'm quiet, she's loud, I'm an introvert, she's an extrovert, I'm a crowd teaser, she's a crowd pleaser, but regardless she's a keeper

For Pat

My boss was more than a boss to me, she was like a mom to me, she had me feeling like I was special you see, she said girl you are really something to me, young, pretty and smart, you remind me of a young version of me, your brilliant you see, you have big dreams, you've conquered so many things, you are destined to be the next big thing, she had me feeling like I could do anything and I'm thankful for her faith in me

For Dre

I am who I am, and I shall be who I want to be, as long as I'm comfortable with me then I will be at peace, your opinion doesn't matter to me because I have to love me

-Auntie Loves you to the moon & back

THOUGHTS

You may have damaged me but God fixed me and I thank you for allowing me to see that I can conquer anything because your destruction has allowed me to continue my construction of me, myself and I so stay tuned.

Many of us our damaged, but God can restore us, mend our hearts and heal our souls. Men may never realize how they affect us but God will never neglect us.

I did it all alone but that didn't stop me from reaching my throne, because when I'm focused I'm in my zone.

My Journey Continues

"I have cleared my eyes of all the tears and cleared my mind of all the fears. The hurt can now go away, I will not allow it to come back not another day in any way. I am done with it, it shall cease and allow me to be free and at relaxing peace as I can now enjoy life and learn to love me."

REALIZE

(This poem was written for an assignment during my first year of college as a reflection of myself) A+

She lives her life according to how others want her to live
she dreams based on the dreams that others have for her
she put's others wants and needs before her own
her life is hers and no one else's
her dreams are hers and no one else's
her wants and needs should come before anyone else's
everyone lives through her
everyone wants her to do what they always wanted to do
pursuing everyone else's dreams,
she never has a chance to pursue her own
putting other's wants and needs before her own
only make's things harder for her

REALIZE cont'd

when will she realize...
her life is her life
her dreams are her dreams
her wants and needs come first, not last
she is beautiful inside and out
she is truly smart
she has a huge heart
some people look up to her, because they envy her
some people look down on her, because they resent her
some people congratulate her, because they love her
this girl is independent
this girl is goal-oriented
this girl is ambitious
she is an all-around people pleaser
when will she realize...
she is extremely beautiful
she is truly smart
she has a huge heart
her father wants her to go to college
her mother wants her to become a model
she wants to become a choreographer

REALIZE cont'd

she went to college
she became a model at the age of 15
she never got a chance to go to dance school
her father is proud
her mother is proud
is she proud?
when will she realize…
she made her father proud
she made her mother proud
she should make herself proud
she lives on her own
she does everything on her own
she works,

she attends college,
she's a mentor,
she is a model,
she can draw,
she can write
when will she realize…
she is independent
she is ambitious
she is talented

REALIZE cont'd

her life is her life
her dreams are her dreams
her wants and needs come first
she is beautiful
she is truly smart
she has a huge heart
she made her father proud
she made her mother proud

she finally realized she is all of the above and some...

WHEN I GO

When I go...

I want people to know

who I was and what I stood for

No matter what they thought

or what they heard

When I'm six feet under

I don't want no one to wonder...

AUTHOR'S COMMENTS

I have been through a lot and I have witnessed a lot
but through it all I have accomplished a lot...
and through the thick and the thin
I will continue to win...

The purpose of my book is to reach out to all of the women and young ladies that have been through tough times and felt that no one could relate to them or understand what they were going through but I am here to tell you that I not only can relate to you, but I understand fully, because I myself have been there. Nevertheless, know you are definitely not alone.

The style that I use when writing my poetry is to tell my story without having to tell the entire story. My poetry is short and sweet so to speak. I allow my readers to decipher the story within the poem. Therefore, as long as you are capable of reading between the lines you will be able to understand my book.

The message that I would like to convey to my readers is that although I have been through hard times, who hasn't; we all have in which I am no different than anyone else. As I have gotten older, I have learned to turn my experiences into stepping stones because they have made me stronger and smarter. Don't let the hard times stop you because without hard times there would be no such thing as good times. My philosophy is; allow the hard times to push you into the good times.

My family and friends always tell me how proud they are of me, and how smart and successful I am, and that is because many of them never knew about my trials and tribulations that is until now, after reading my book. I held these things in for so long. All they have really known about are my accomplishments because I am constantly pushing myself to reach my goals and to be successful. God has truly blessed me, therefore I thank him for my hard times as well as my good times because those hard times brought me to better times. This book is my therapy, it was time for me to get rid of all of my hurt and pain because hurt and pain can hold you from your full potential and in order to move on you have to let go. And, although, I don't disclose all of my life's troubles, struggles and obstacles, the ones I do tell are proof enough of my testimony and my strength.

God continues to bless me each and every day and in every way.

This book is not only a reflection of my life but it is a reflection of the experiences of many women and young girls. In writing this book, I want to express to them that no matter how much you've been through you can still succeed and accomplish your dreams.

If I can do it, you can too!

In many of my poems, I leave you wondering what the outcome was but you actually already know the outcome to every poem…and that is, I'm still here, I'm still breathing and living, growing and learning, staying blessed and unstressed.

ABOUT THE AUTHOR

Krystal Galatia Steward was born in Wayne Michigan. Krystal's parents divorced when she was about 6 years old and both remarried when she was eight years old. Krystal has one sibling, an older brother.

Throughout her childhood Krystal spent a lot of time with her grandparents. Krystal was raised in church and proclaims her love for the Lord.

Krystal began working with her grandfather at the tender age of nine. She worked with him during the summer months, selling elephant ears (a pastry desert) and face painting at festivals throughout Michigan which taught her independence and responsibility at a young age. At the age of fourteen she started her first real job as an usher at a movie theatre and she has not stopped working since.

Ms. Steward began modeling at the age of fifteen and owns the nickname of MODELKSTEW. In 2005 she was a contestant in the Michigan Sunburst Beauty Pageant at the age of twenty two. Ms. Steward proudly gave birth to her son, Keyair at the age of twenty three.

Krystal began working in the housing field in 2004, her love for people and helping others is what led her to switch her major in college from Criminal Justice to Social Work. That position involved working with different populations within the community. This was a perfect setting for Krystal who has always been able to make friends due to her kind, caring, friendly, and loving nature. Furthermore, she was a mentor for Big Brothers, Big Sisters for three and a half years. Ms. Steward also successfully accomplished starting her own business at twenty six.

Damaged But Not Broken

In May of 2007 Krystal was diagnosed with an Osteoma bone tumor on her head. It had been mis-diagnosed several times over the years. By the grace of God, two weeks later, after the final diagnoses was made, surgery was performed and the biopsy came back negative for cancer.

A year later in May of 2008 Krystal received her Associate's degree in Human Services and three years later in June of 2011, she went on to receive her Bachelor's degree in Human Services Management.

Today Ms. Steward continues to work in the housing field as a Social Worker, holds several professional licenses and is well known within her community. She is currently working towards completing her Master's degree in Educational Psychology. Ms. Steward continues to excel in life through faith and growth and in 2014 she reached an ultimate goal by purchasing her first home at the age of 30 for herself and her son.

Ms. Steward is a simple gal, who in her spare time enjoys spending time with family (her immediate as well as her extended family), drawing, arts and crafts, playing video and board games, writing, reading, dancing, traveling, horse-back riding, modeling and watching movies.

Shortly before her 28th birthday in 2010 as a result of her wake-up call (last domestic violence incident) Krystal wrote her first book. Some of the poems in this book were written when Ms. Steward was an adolescent as well as in her early 20's. A couple of Ms. Steward's poems were winners in national poetry contests and can be found in the poetry.com poet database.

Ms. Steward has waited 6 long years before finally deciding to publish her book and share her story with the world. Over the past 6 years she has made several versions of her book, adding and removing various poems. But now, she exclaims, it is finally ready.

Stay Tuned for more from Ms. Steward…

In 2014 Ms. Steward created a woman's group called "Our Story Woman's Group" via social media and plans to soon incorporate formal monthly meetings for members to connect in a personal setting. The group was created as a place for woman to open up about their struggles and experiences with others who can relate to them and won't judge them; because at the end of the day we all have a story, a struggle and a testimony.

For more information visit:
www.facebook.com/AuthorKrystalSteward
and/or
contact authorkrystalgsteward@gmail.com

Ms. Steward is available for speaking engagements and book signings!

Damaged But Not Broken

KRYSTAL STEWARD

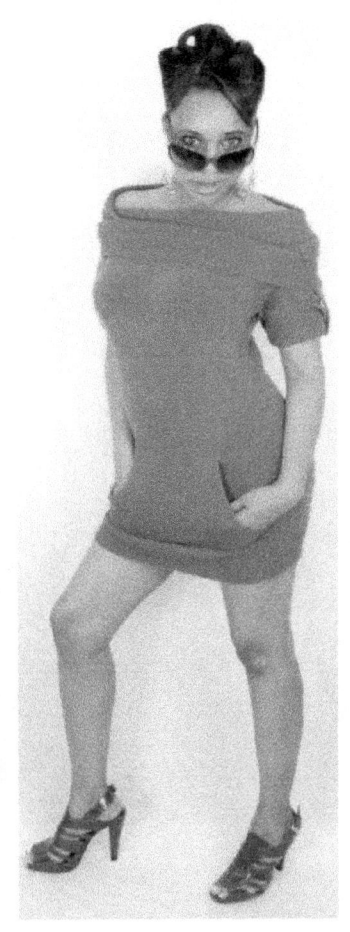

KRYSTAL STEWARD

KRYSTAL STEWARD

KRYSTAL STEWARD

KRYSTAL STEWARD

KRYSTAL STEWARD

KRYSTAL STEWARD

KRYSTAL STEWARD

KRYSTAL STEWARD

KRYSTAL STEWARD

KRYSTAL STEWARD

KRYSTAL STEWARD

GOD BLESS!

KRYSTAL STEWARD

www.ingramcontent.com/pod-product-compliance
Lightning Source LLC
Chambersburg PA
CBHW032001080426
42735CB00007B/463